Favorite Standards

By Jeff Arnold

ISBN-13: 978-1-4234-0588-7

ISBN-10: 1-4234-0588-9

HAL•LEONARD®
CORPORATION

7777 W. BLUEMOUND RD. P.O. BOX 13819 MILWAUKEE, WI 53213

Visit Hal Leonard Online at **www.halleonard.com**

All the Way

from THE JOKER IS WILD
Words by Sammy Cahn
Music by James Van Heusen

Autumn in New York

Words and Music by Vernon Duke

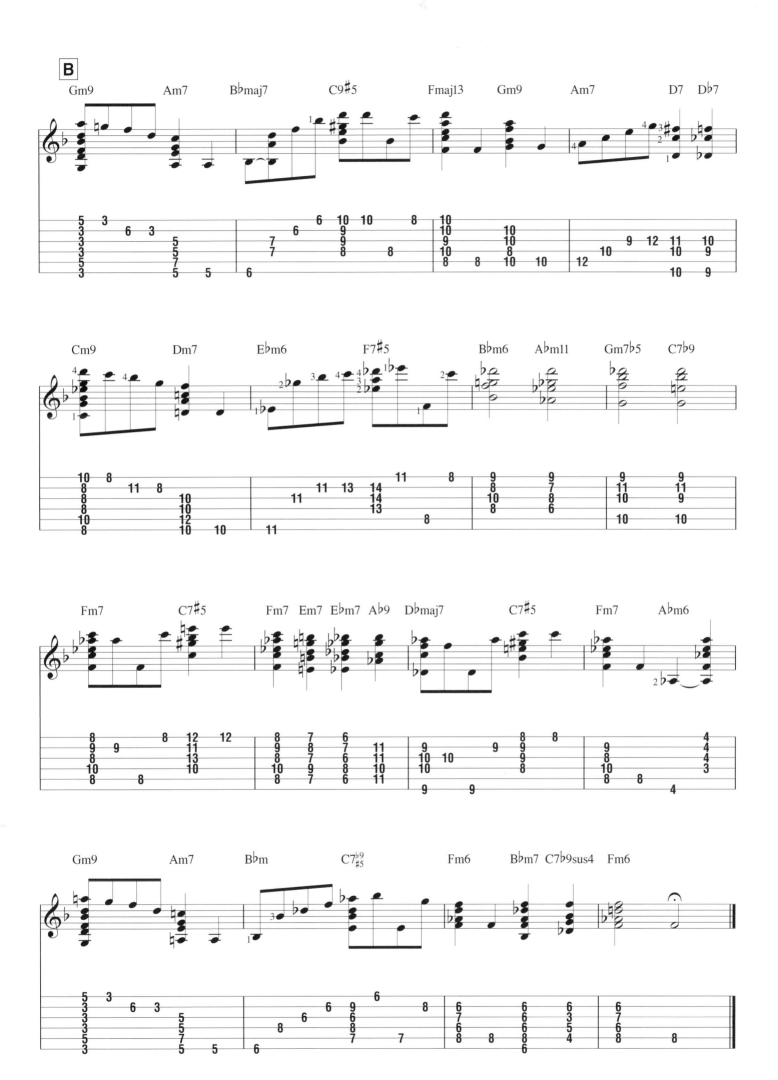

Autumn Leaves

English lyric by Johnny Mercer
French lyric by Jacques Prevert
Music by Joseph Kosma

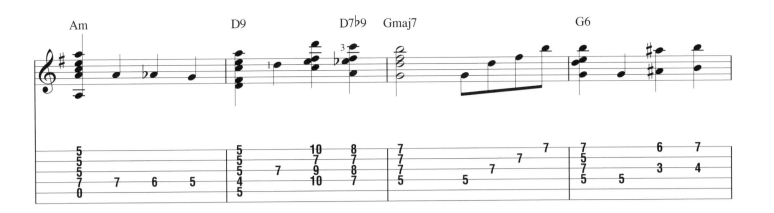

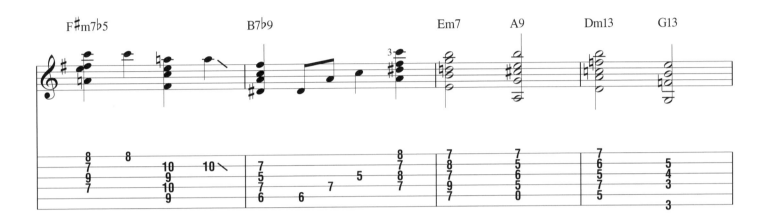

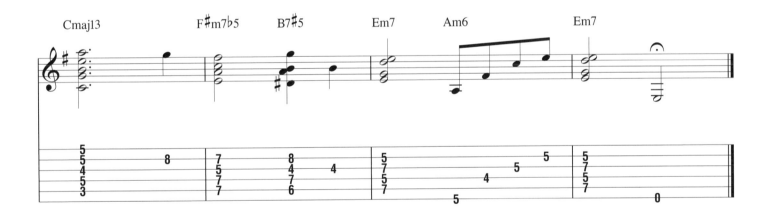

The Birth of the Blues

from GEORGE WHITE'S SCANDALS OF 1926

Words by B.G. DeSylva and Lew Brown
Music by Ray Henderson

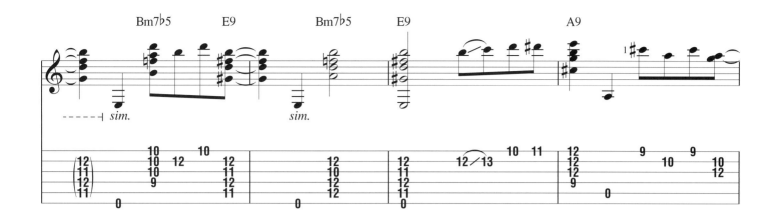

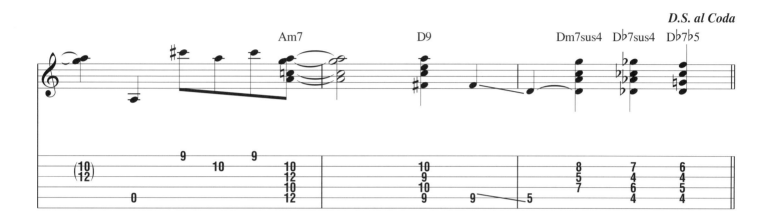

Coda

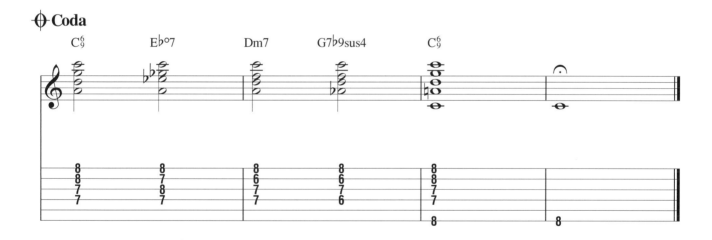

9

Blue Skies

from BETSY
featured in BLUE SKIES
Words and Music by Irving Berlin

Cheek to Cheek

from the RKO Radio Motion Picture TOP HAT

Words and Music by Irving Berlin

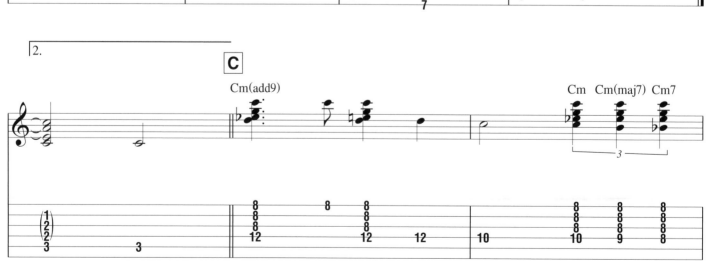

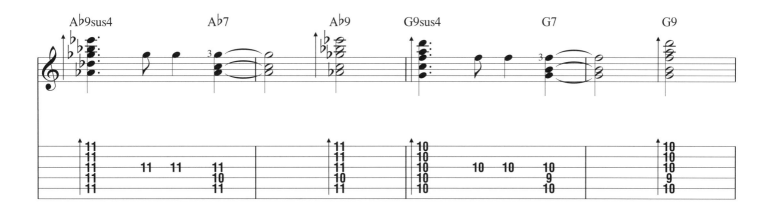

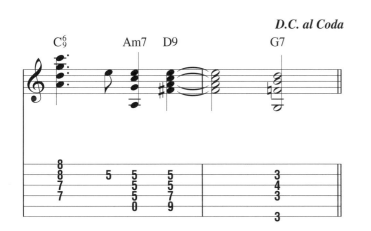

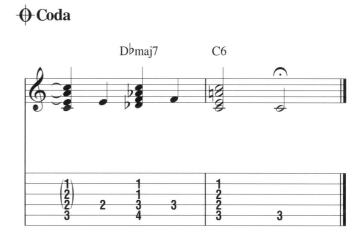

Can't Help Lovin' Dat Man

from SHOW BOAT

Lyrics by Oscar Hammerstein II
Music by Jerome Kern

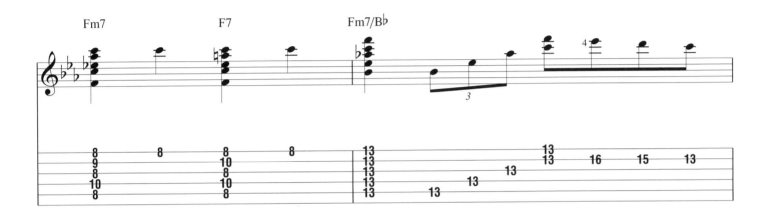

Coda

D.C. al Coda

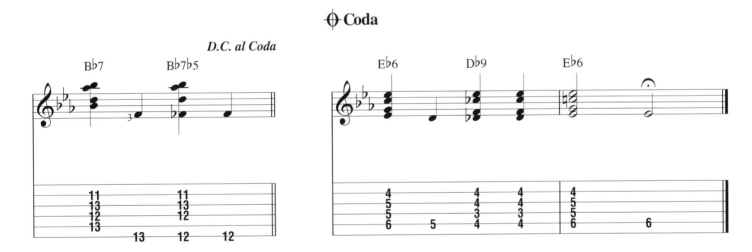

Don't Get Around Much Anymore

from SOPHISTICATED LADY

Words and Music by Duke Ellington and Bob Russell

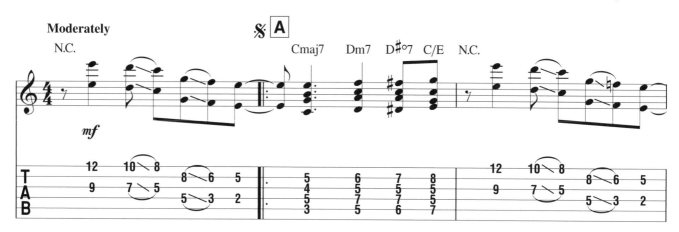

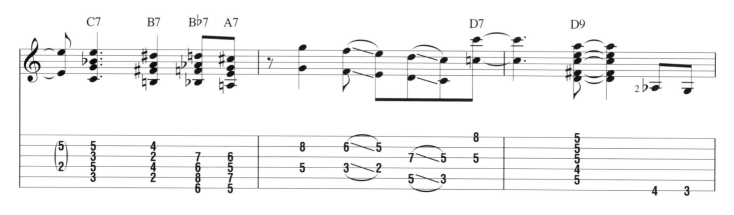

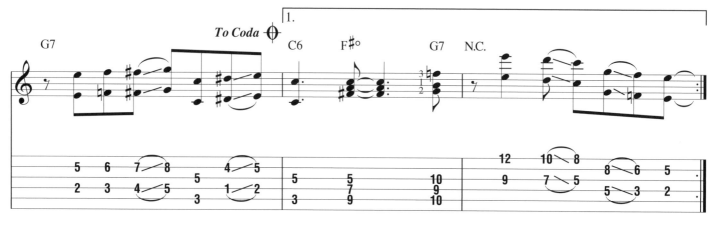

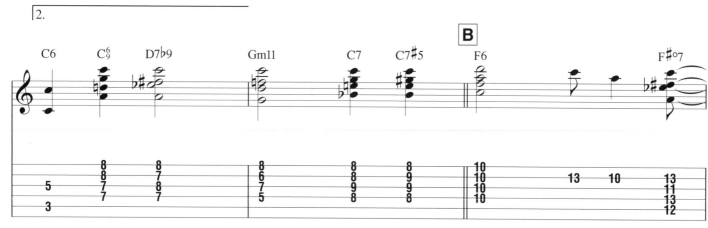

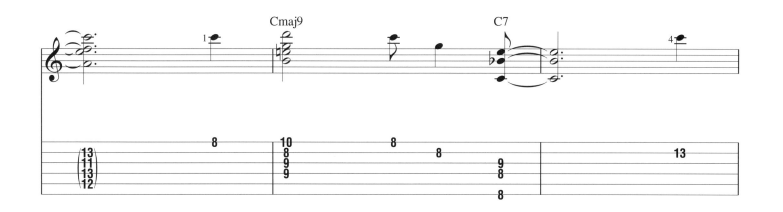

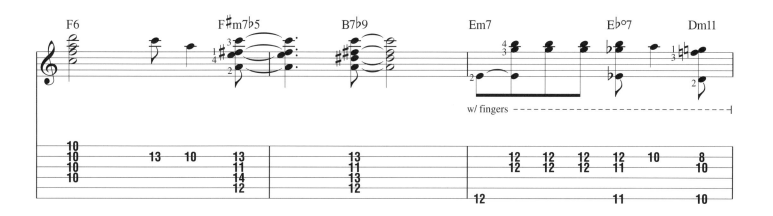

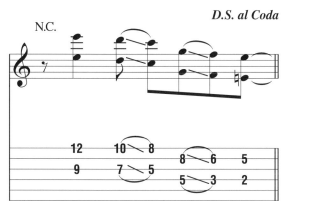

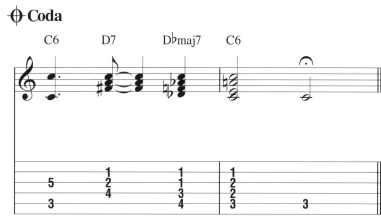

Falling in Love With Love

from THE BOYS FROM SYRACUSE

Words by Lorenz Hart
Music by Richard Rodgers

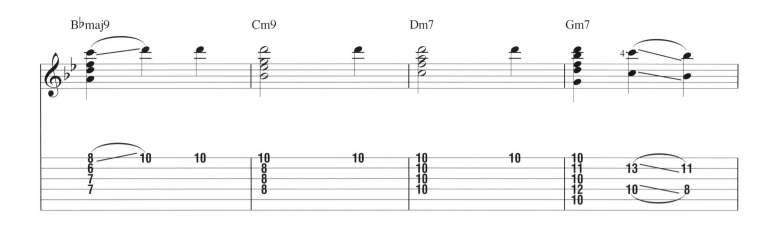

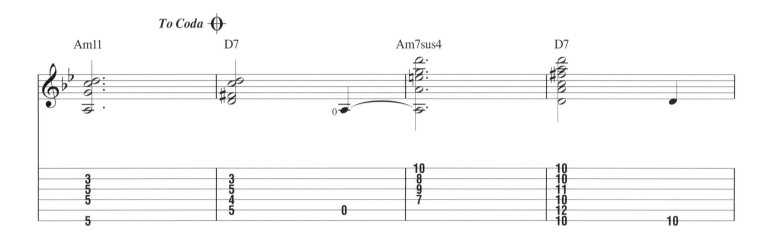

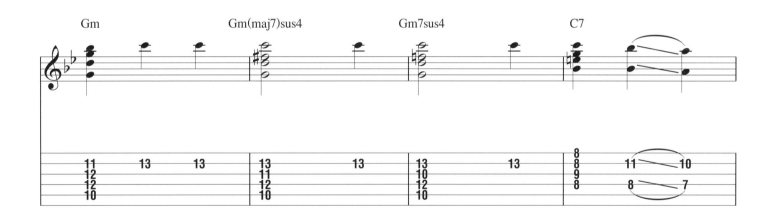

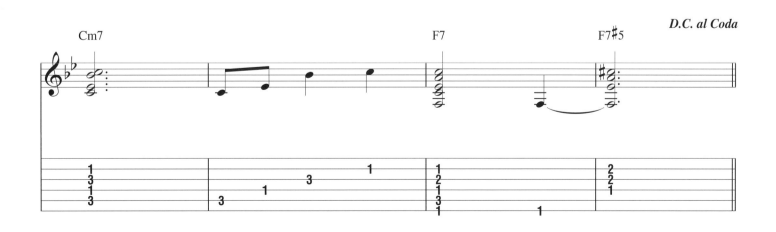

⊕ Coda

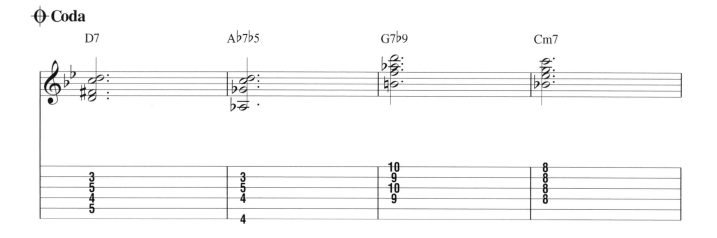

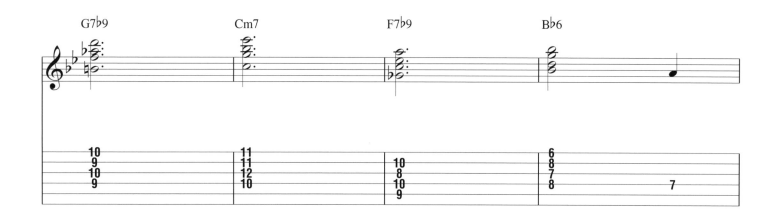

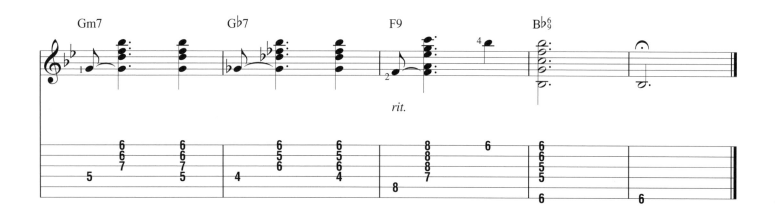

I'll Remember April

Words and Music by Pat Johnson, Don Raye and Gene De Paul

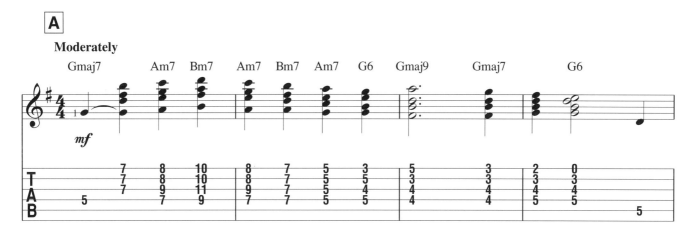

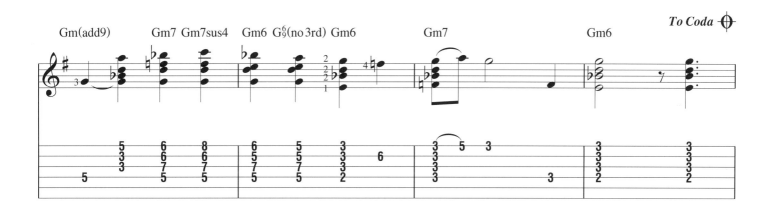

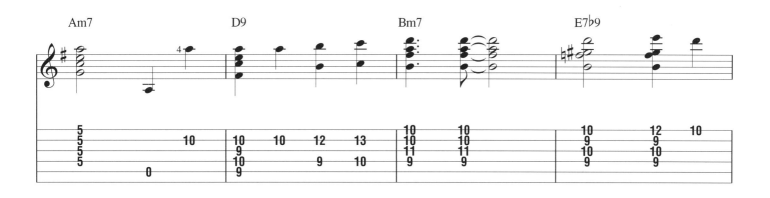

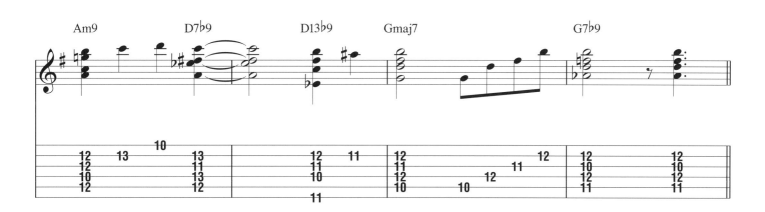

B

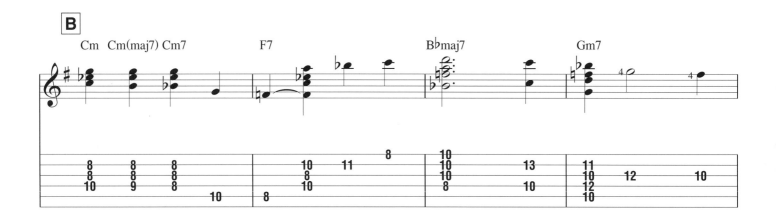

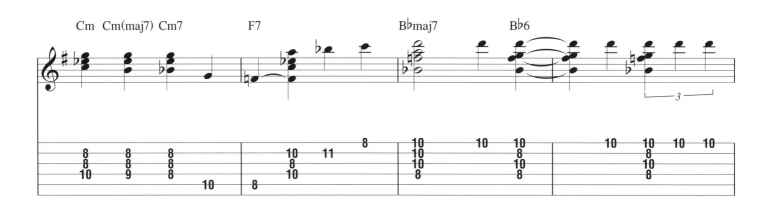

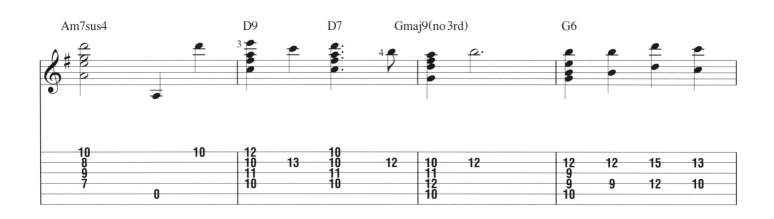

D.C. al Coda

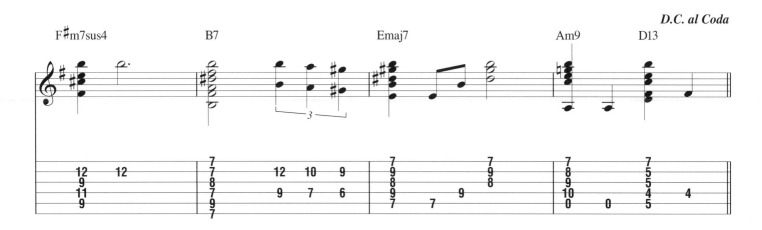

22

⊕ Coda

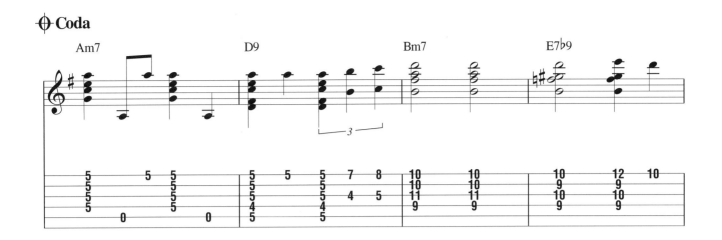

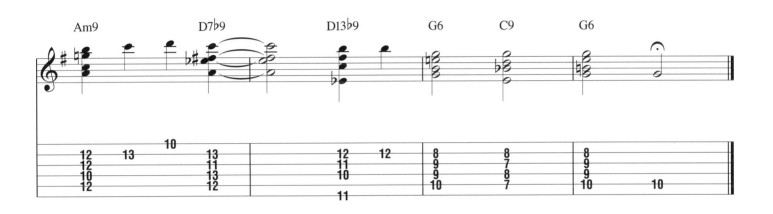

How Deep Is the Ocean

(How High Is the Sky)

Words and Music by Irving Berlin

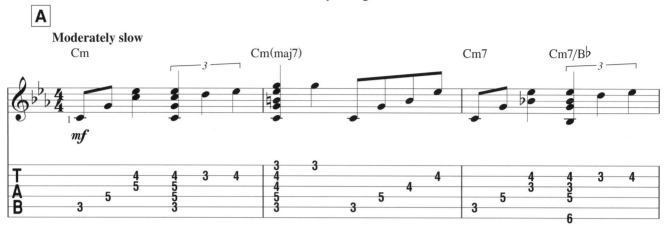

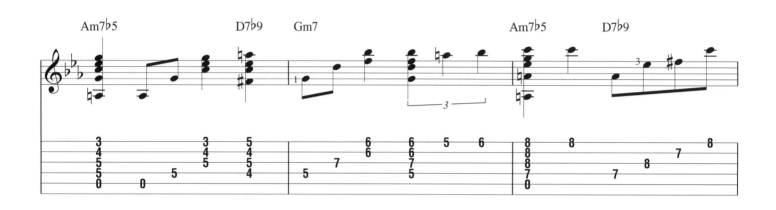

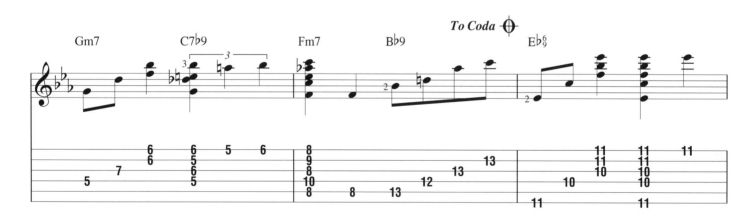

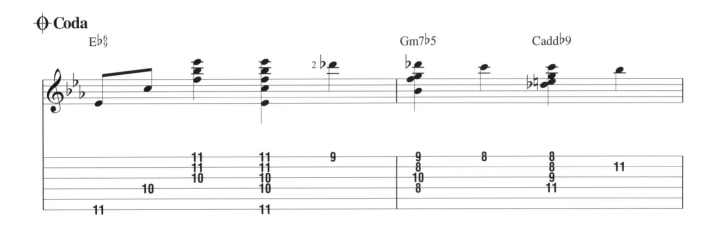

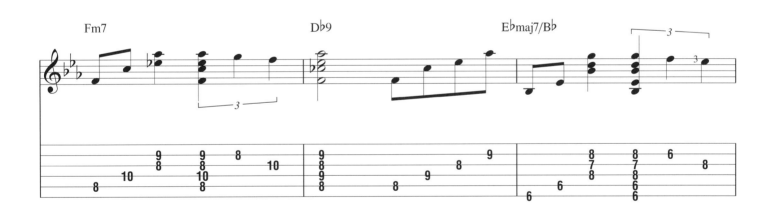

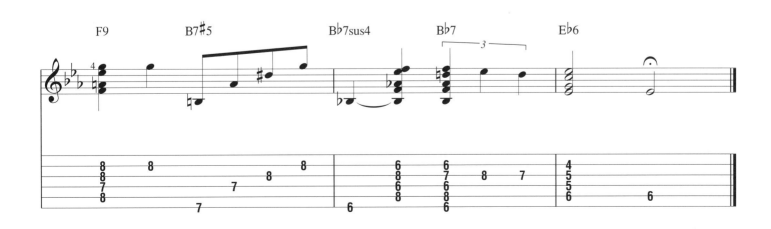

I'll Be Seeing You

from RIGHT THIS WAY

Lyric by Irving Kahal
Music by Sammy Fain

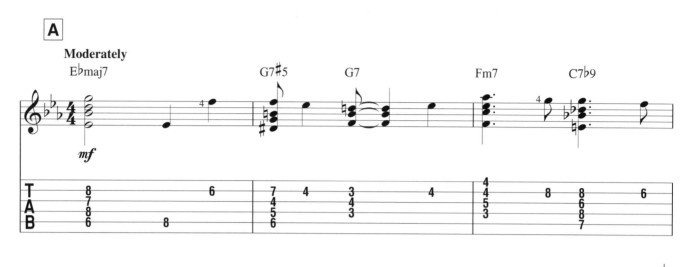

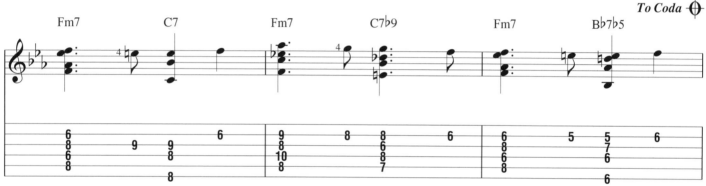

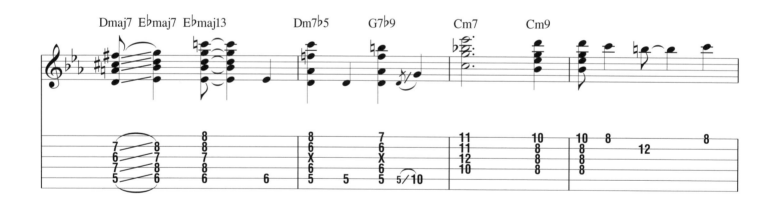

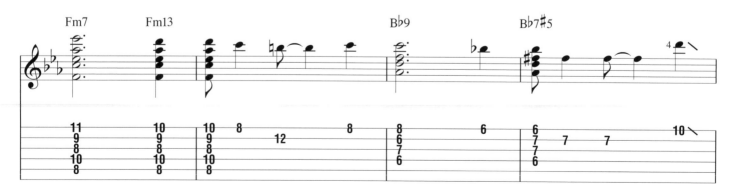

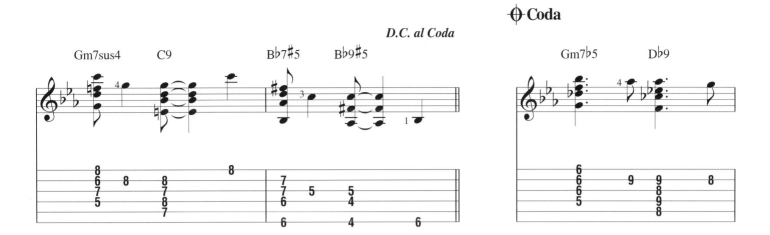

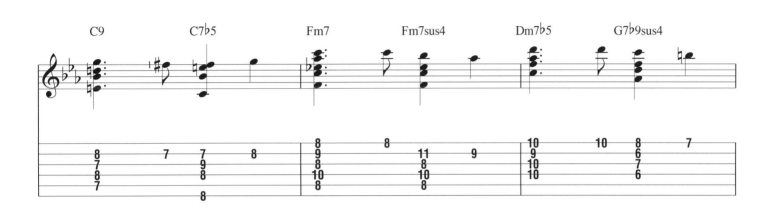

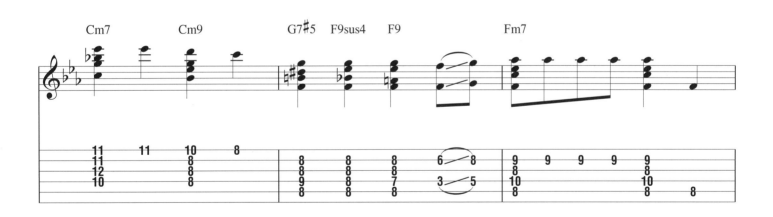

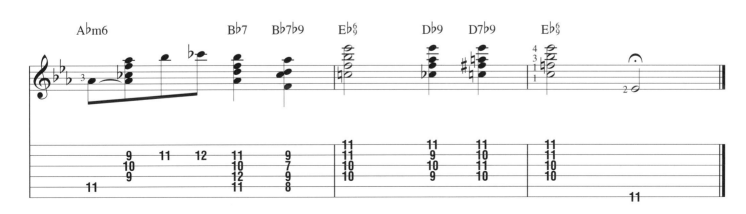

I've Got the World on a String

Lyric by Ted Koehler
Music by Harold Arlen

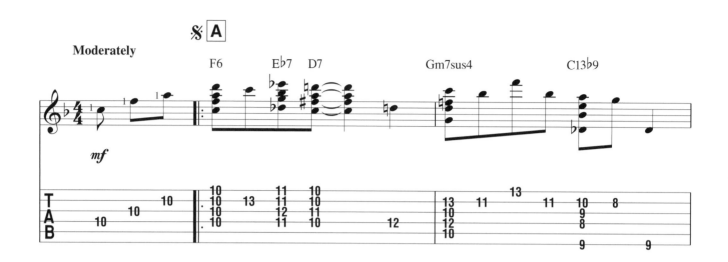

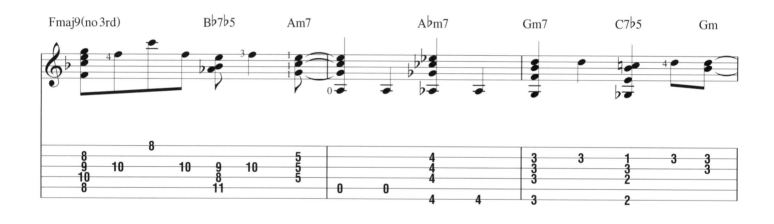

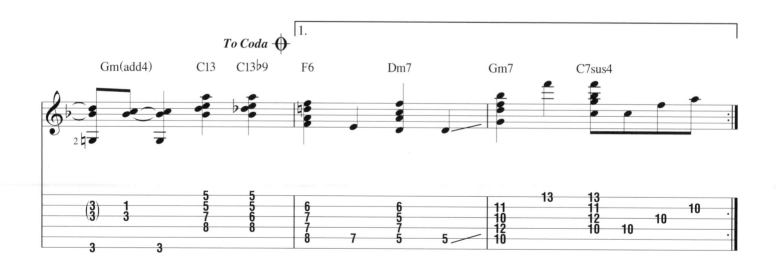

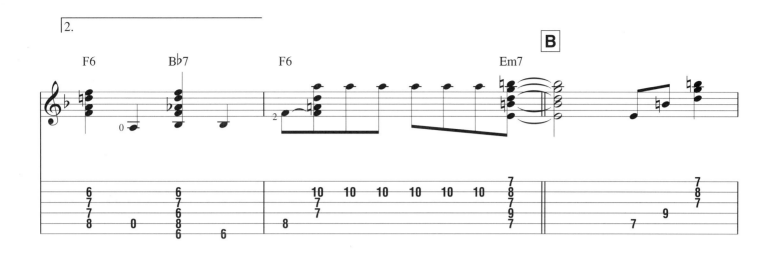

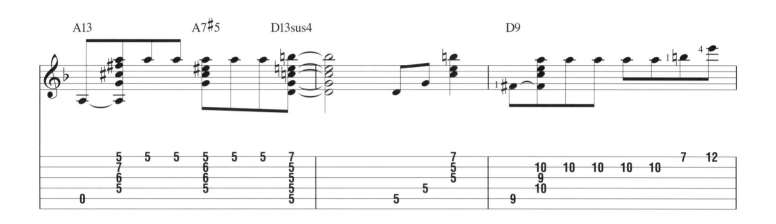

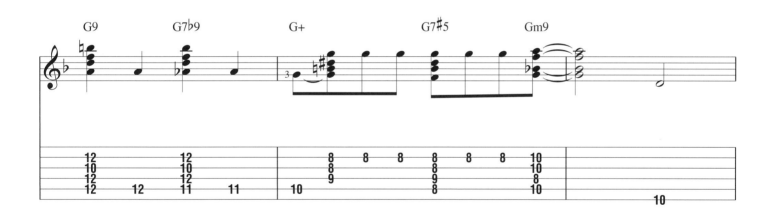

⊕ Coda

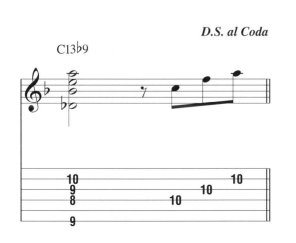

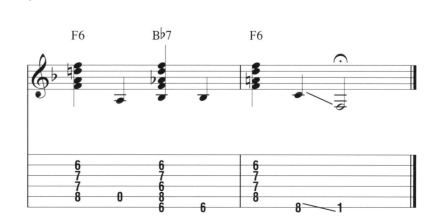

If I Should Lose You

from the Paramount Picture ROSE OF THE RANCHO

Words and Music by Leo Robin and Ralph Rainger

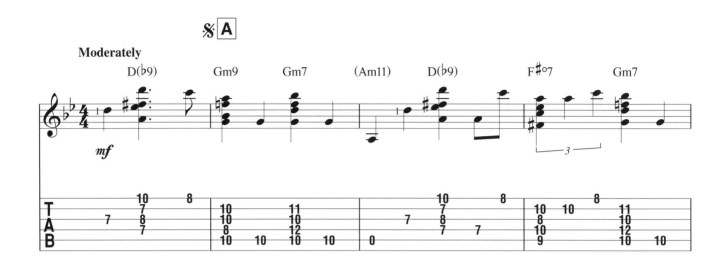

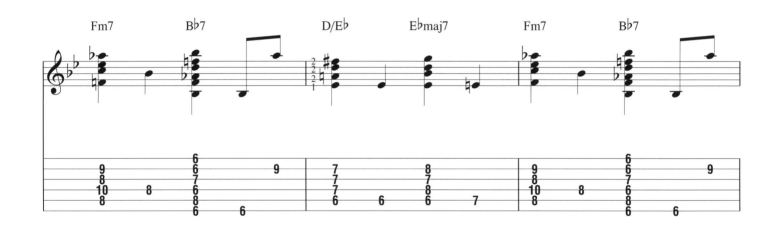

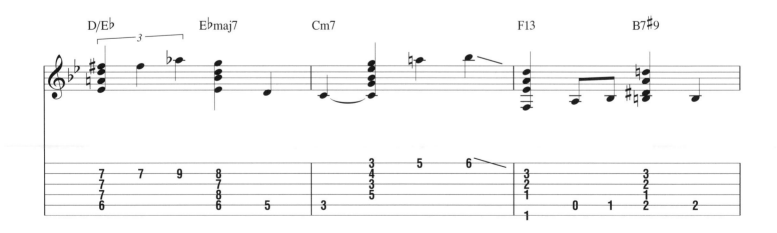

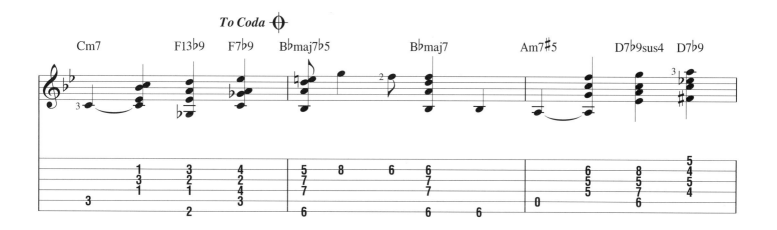

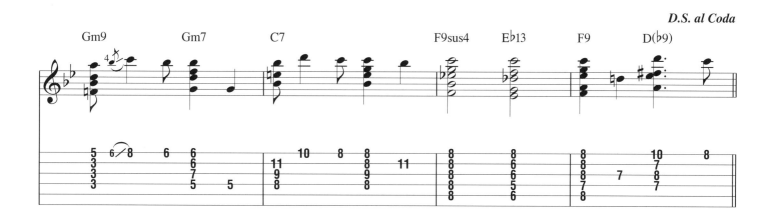

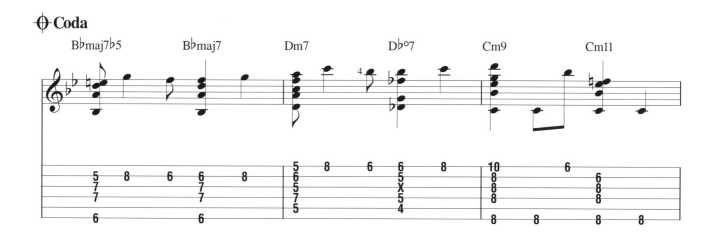

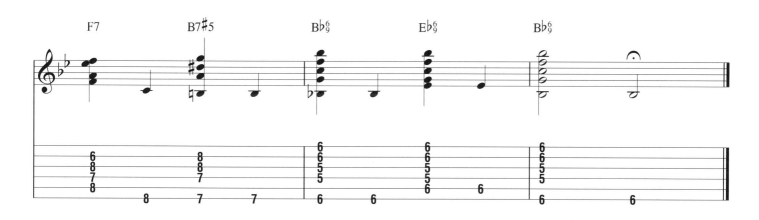

If I Were a Bell

from GUYS AND DOLLS

By Frank Loesser

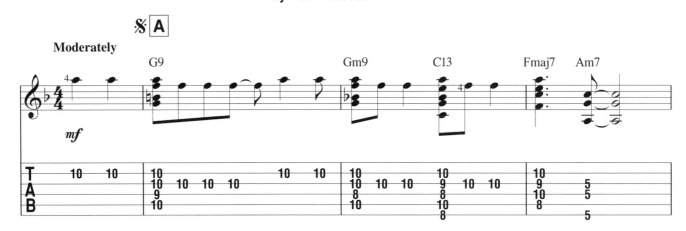

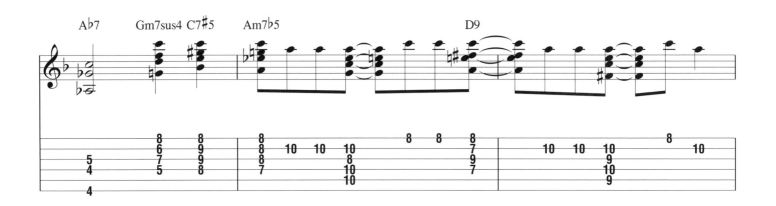

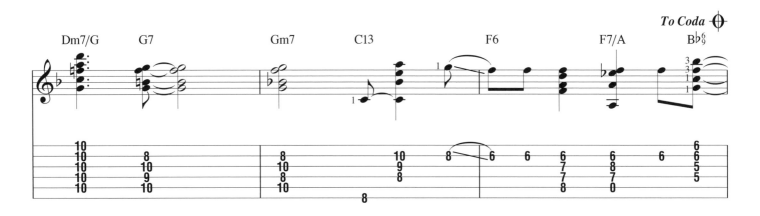

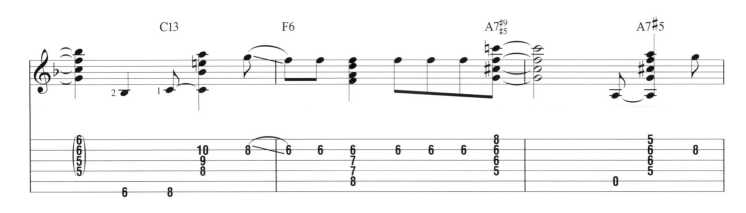

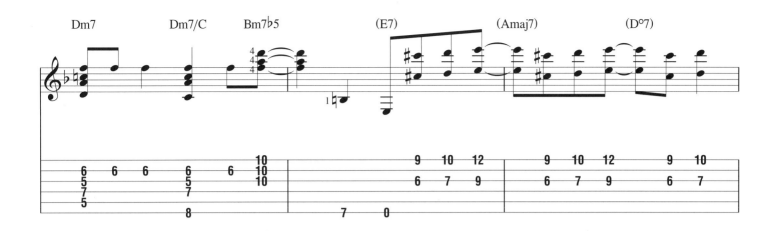

Coda

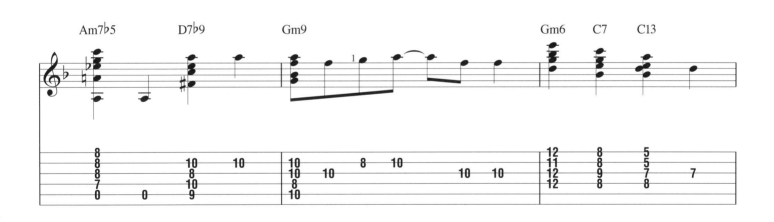

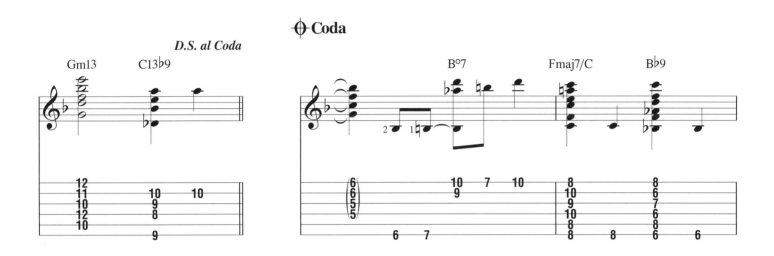

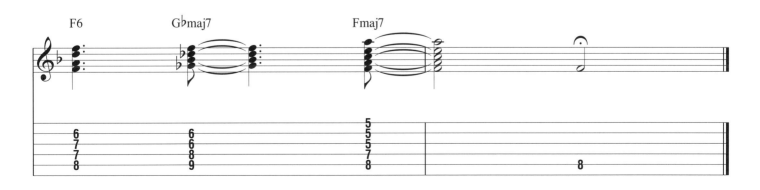

Isn't It Romantic?

from the Paramount Picture LOVE ME TONIGHT

Words by Lorenz Hart
Music by Richard Rodgers

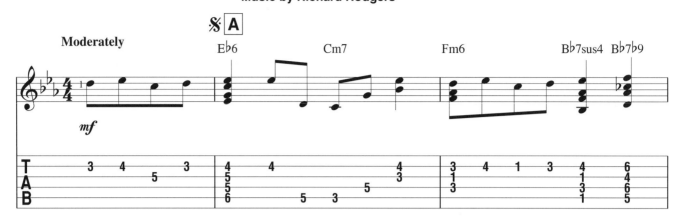

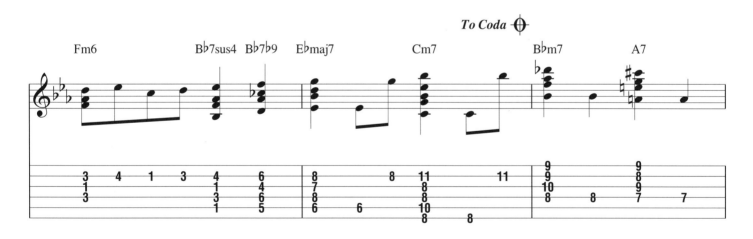

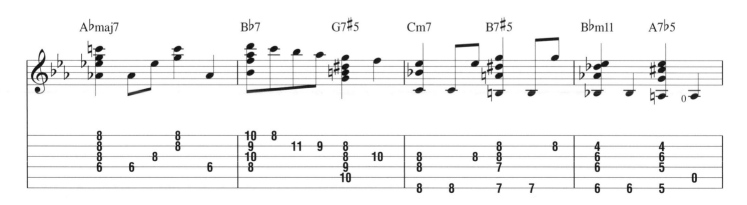

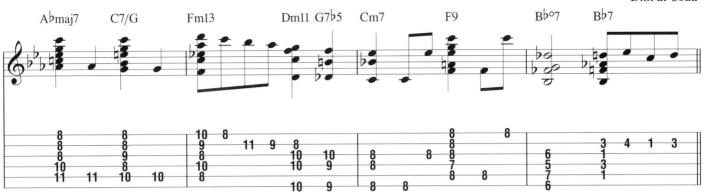

Coda

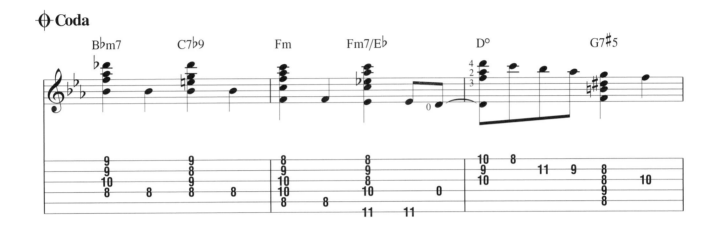

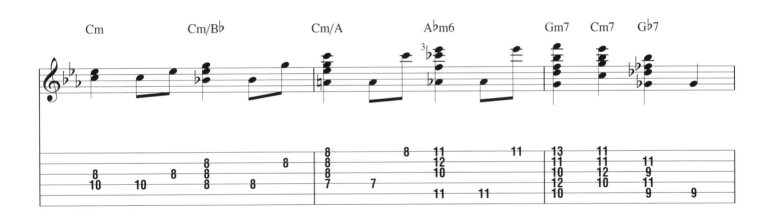

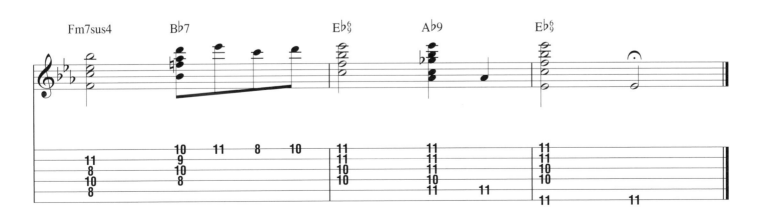

It Could Happen to You

from the Paramount Picture AND THE ANGELS SING
Words by Johnny Burke
Music by James Van Heusen

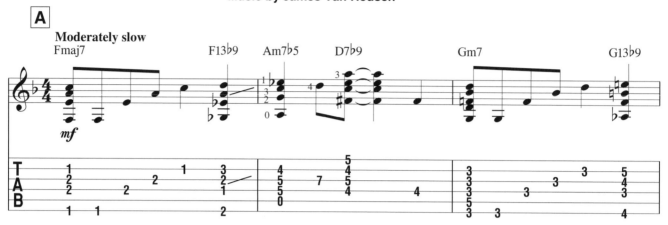

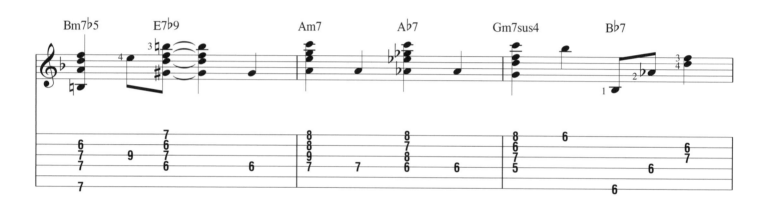

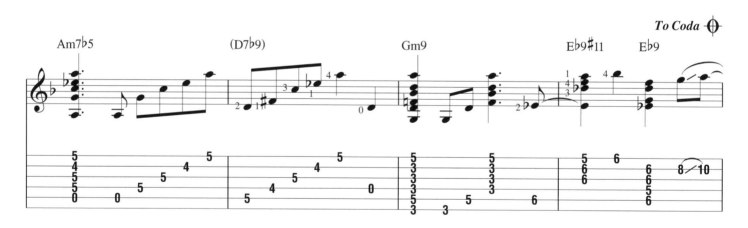

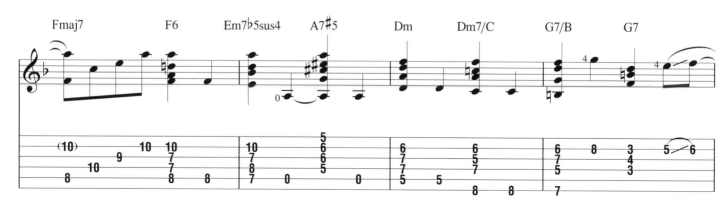

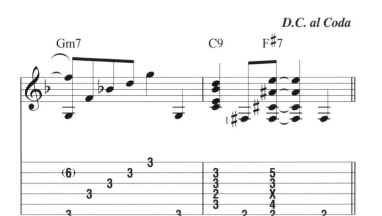

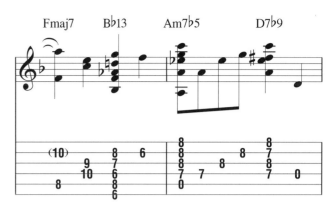

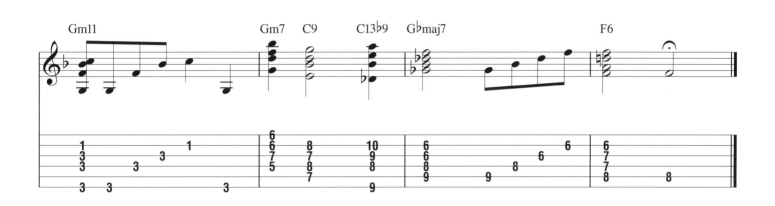

The Lady Is a Tramp

from BABES IN ARMS
from WORDS AND MUSIC

Words by Lorenz Hart
Music by Richard Rodgers

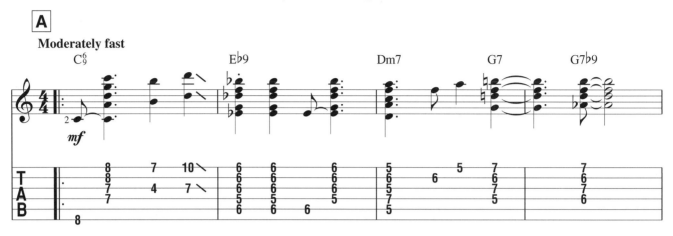

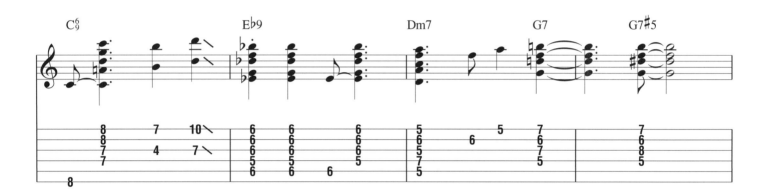

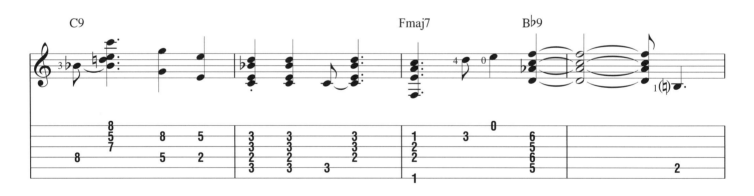

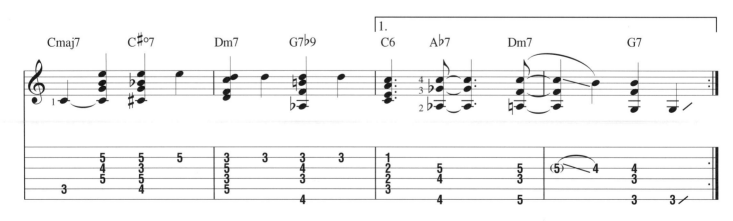

Moon River

from the Paramount Picture BREAKFAST AT TIFFANY'S
Words by Johnny Mercer
Music by Henry Mancini

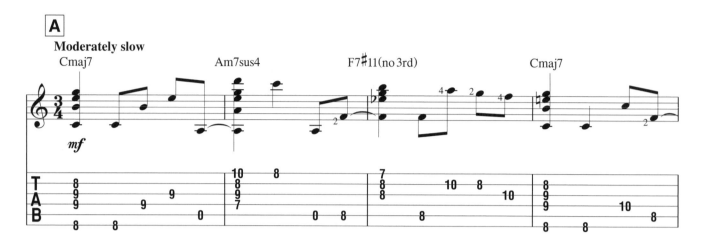

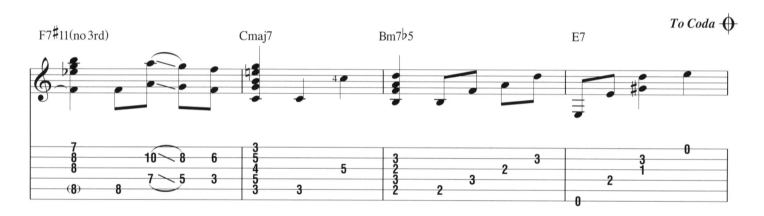

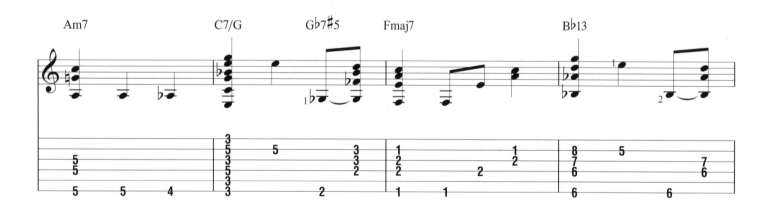

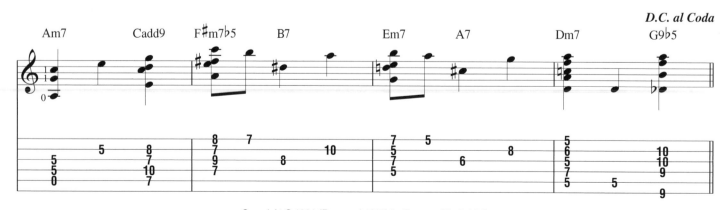

⊕ Coda

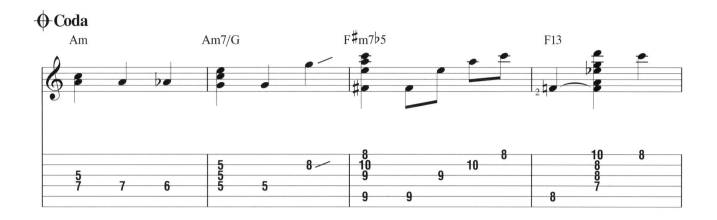

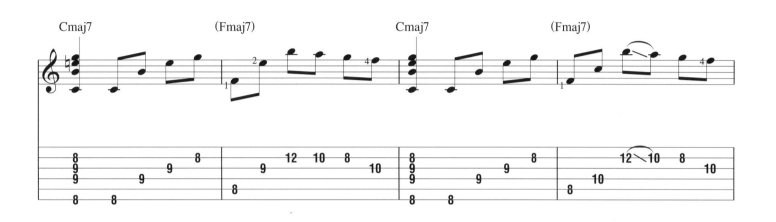

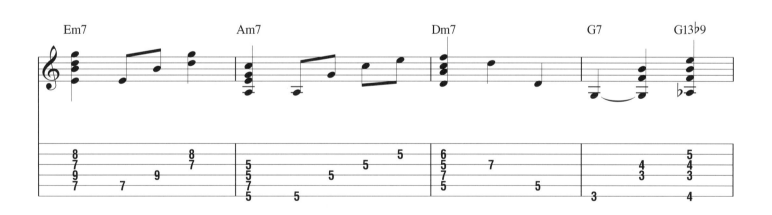

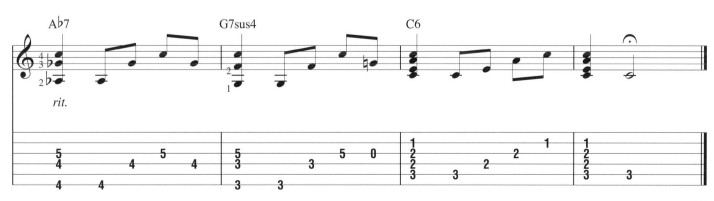

My Ship

from the Musical Production LADY IN THE DARK
Words by Ira Gershwin
Music by Kurt Weill

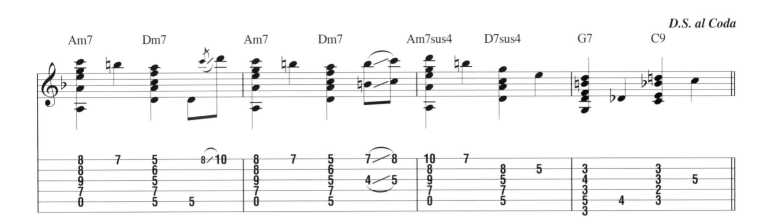

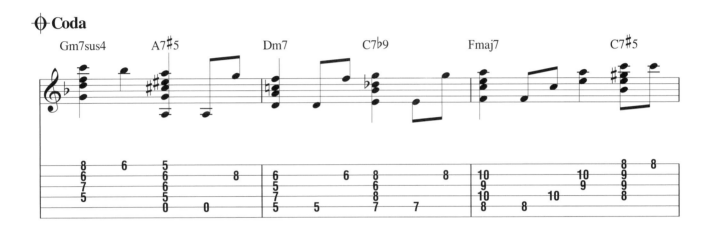

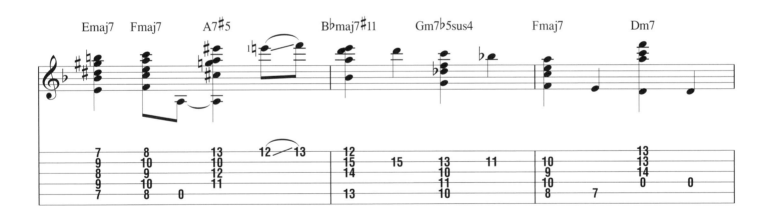

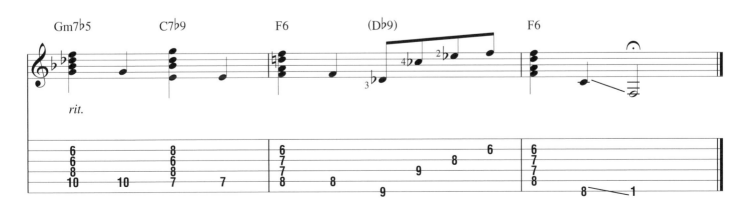

Speak Low

from the Musical Production ONE TOUCH OF VENUS
Words by Ogden Nash
Music by Kurt Weill

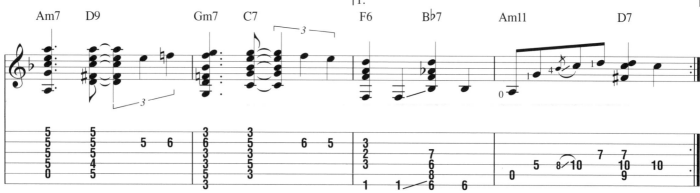

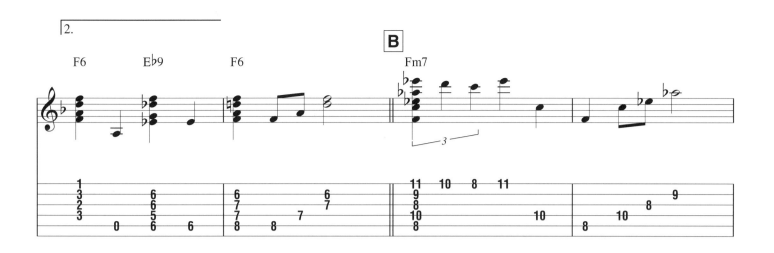

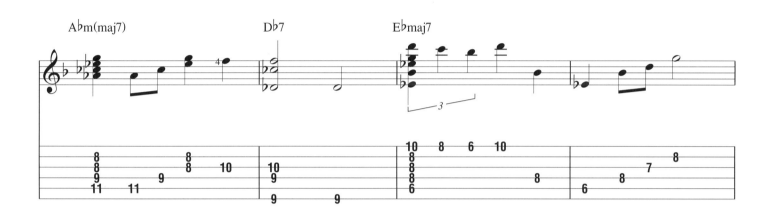

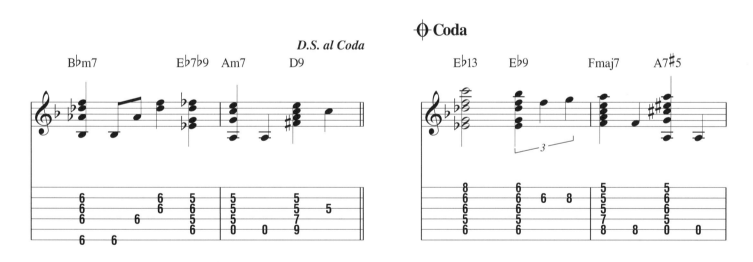

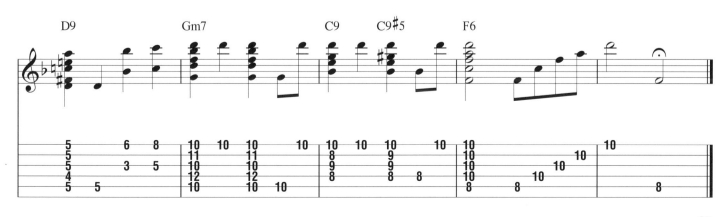

Stardust

Words by Mitchell Parish
Music by Hoagy Carmichael

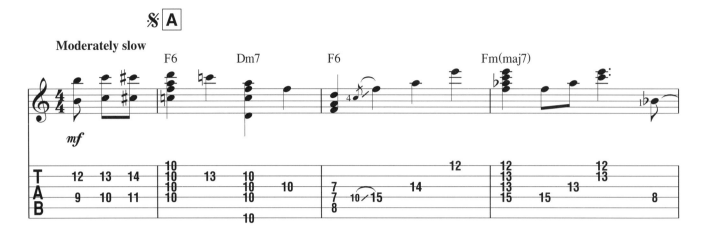

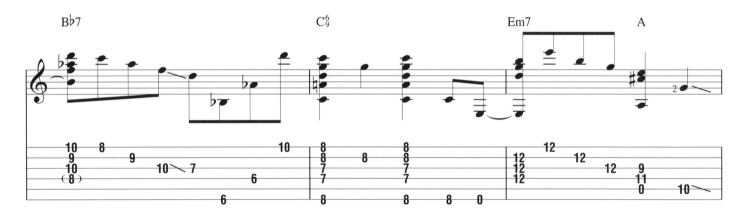

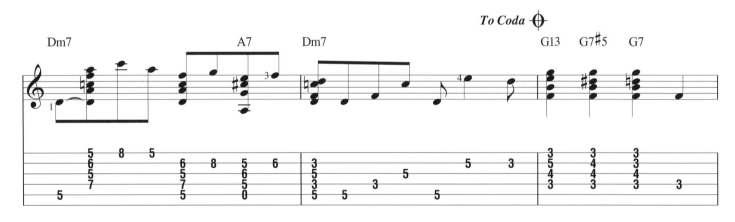

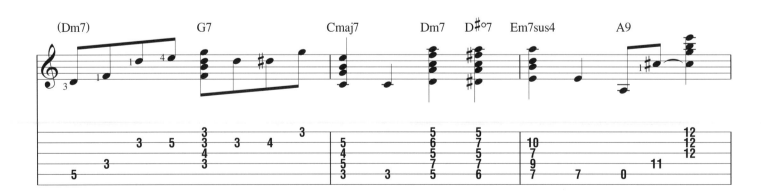

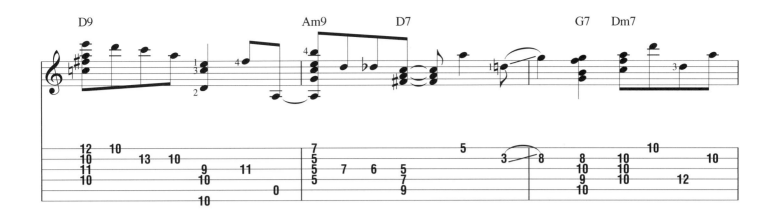

Coda

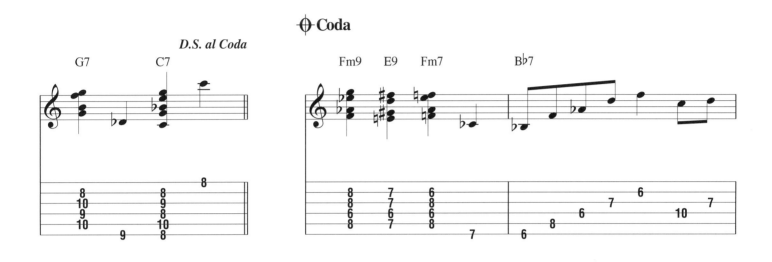

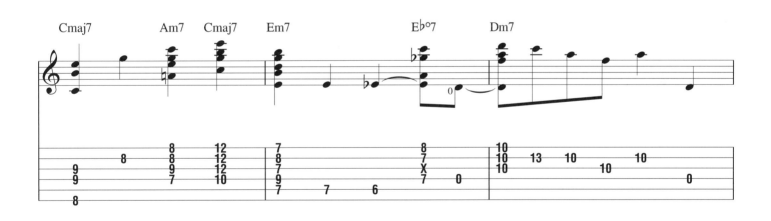

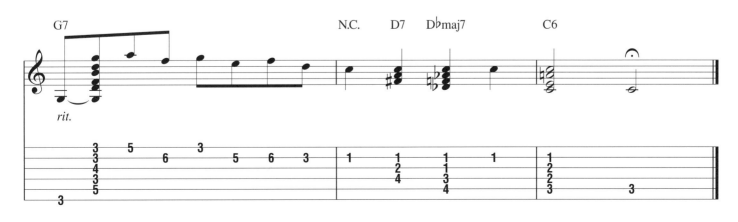

Tangerine

from the Paramount Picture THE FLEET'S IN
Words by Johnny Mercer
Music by Victor Schertzinger

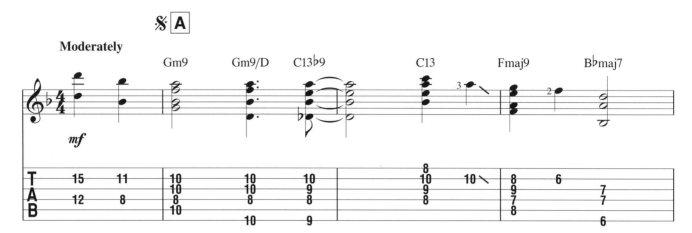

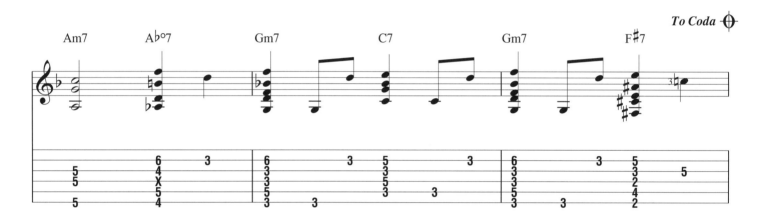

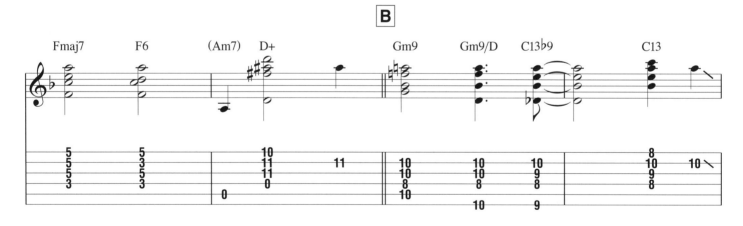

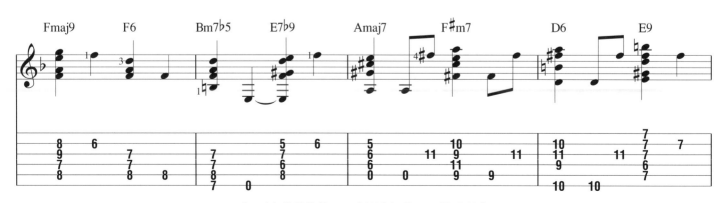

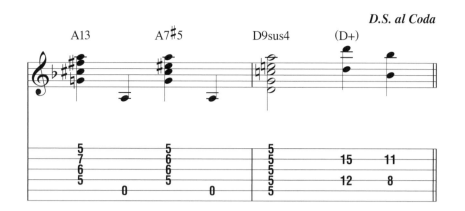

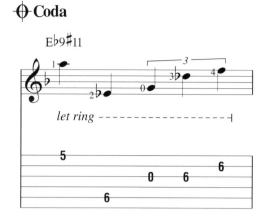

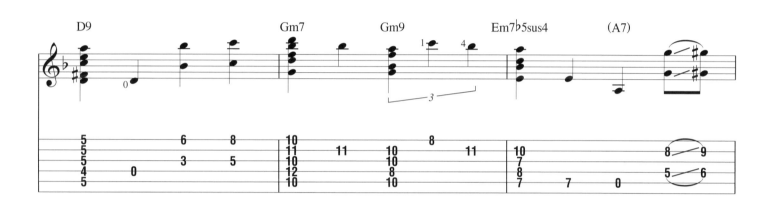

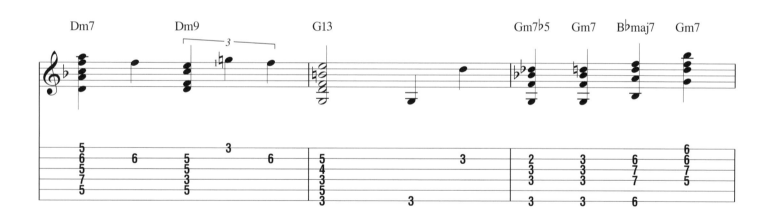

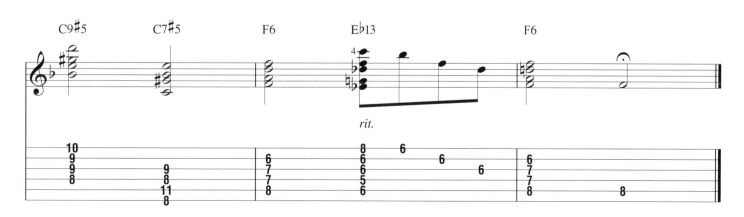

(Love Is) The Tender Trap

Words by Sammy Cahn
Music by James Van Heusen

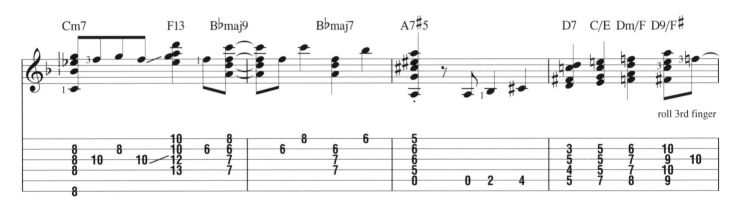

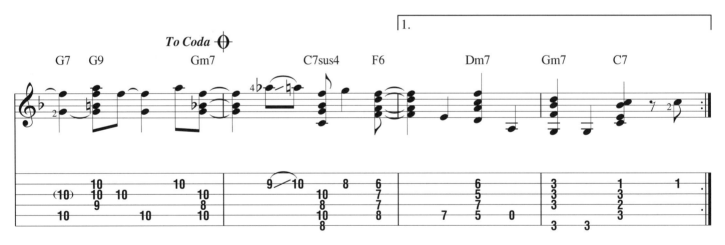

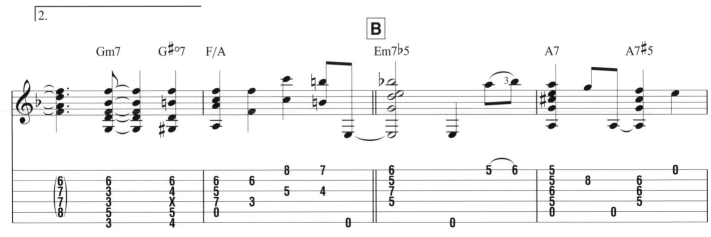

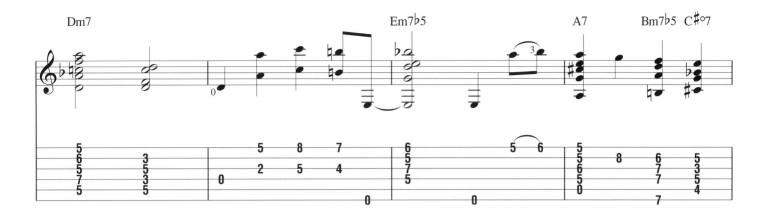

Coda

D.S. al Coda

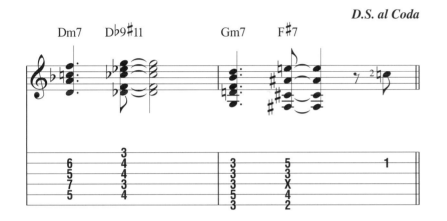

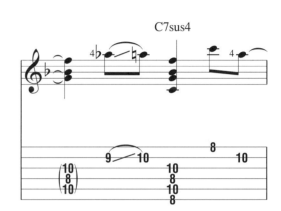

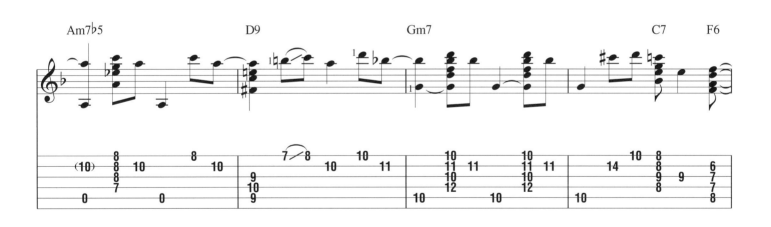

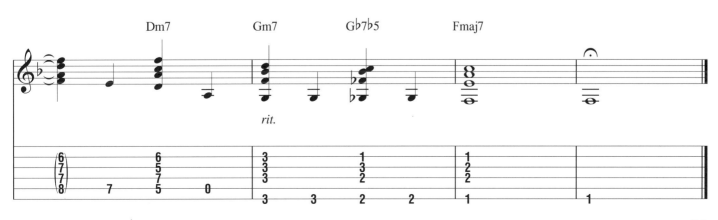

Willow Weep for Me

Words and Music by Ann Ronell

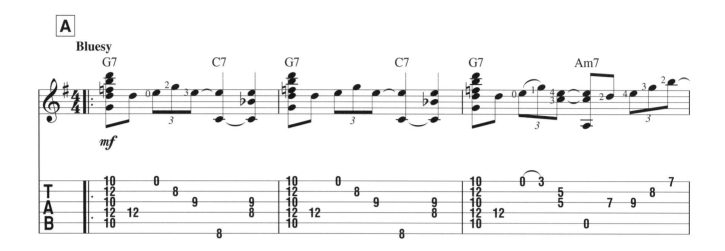

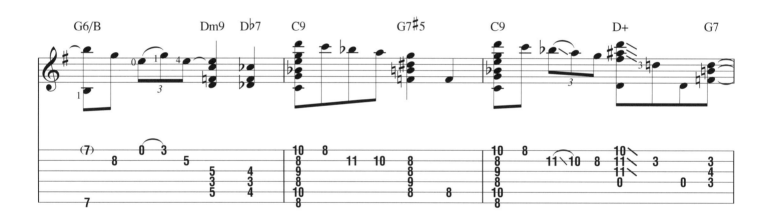

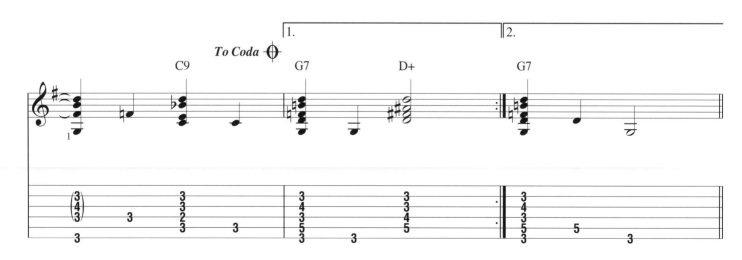

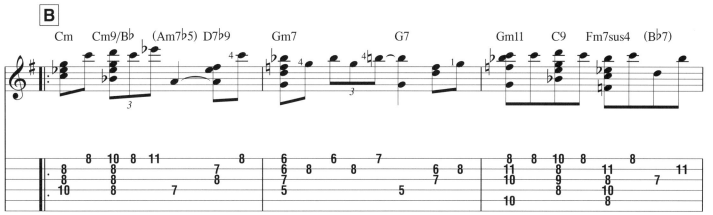

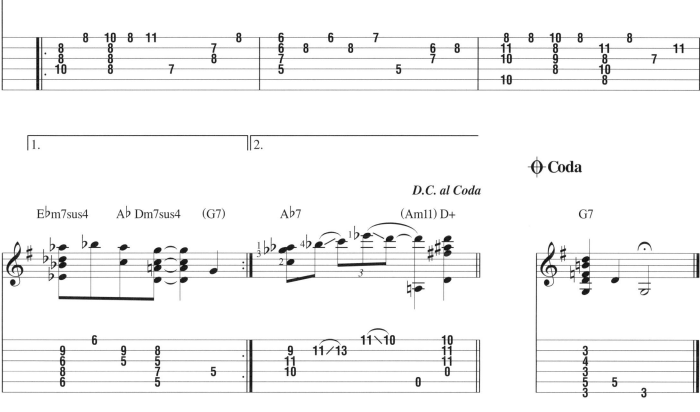

Witchcraft

Lyric by Carolyn Leigh
Music by Cy Coleman

Take the "A" Train

Words and Music by Billy Strayhorn